AARON RODGERS

Tammy Gagne

Mitchell Lane
PUBLISHERS

P.O. Box 196
Hockessin, Delaware 19707
Visit us on the web: www.mitchelllane.com
Comments? Email us: mitchelllane@mitchelllane.com

Mitchell Lane
PUBLISHERS

Printing   1   2   3   4   5   6   7   8   9

A Robbie Reader Biography

Aaron Rodgers	Drake Bell & Josh Peck	LeBron James
Abigail Breslin	Dr. Seuss	Mia Hamm
Adrian Peterson	Dwayne "The Rock" Johnson	Michael Strahan
Albert Einstein	Dwyane Wade	Miley Cyrus
Albert Pujols	Dylan & Cole Sprouse	Miranda Cosgrove
Alex Rodriguez	Eli Manning	Philo Farnsworth
Aly and AJ	Emily Osment	Raven-Symoné
Amanda Bynes	Emma Watson	Roy Halladay
AnnaSophia Robb	Hilary Duff	Selena Gomez
Ashley Tisdale	Jaden Smith	Shaquille O'Neal
Brenda Song	Jamie Lynn Spears	Story of Harley-Davidson
Brittany Murphy	Jennette McCurdy	Sue Bird
Carmelo Anthony	Jeremy Lin	Syd Hoff
Charles Schulz	Jesse McCartney	Taylor Lautner
Chris Johnson	Jimmie Johnson	Tiki Barber
Cliff Lee	Johnny Gruelle	Tim Lincecum
Dakota Fanning	Jonas Brothers	Tom Brady
Dale Earnhardt Jr.	Jordin Sparks	Tony Hawk
David Archuleta	Justin Beiber	Troy Polamalu
Debby Ryan	Keke Palmer	Tyler Perry
Demi Lovato	Larry Fitzgerald	Victoria Justice
Donovan McNabb		

Library of Congress Cataloging-in-Publication Data
Gagne, Tammy.
 Aaron Rodgers / by Tammy Gagne.
     p. cm. — (A Robbie Reader)
 Includes bibliographical references and index.
 ISBN 978-1-61228-330-2 (library bound)
 1. Rodgers, Aaron, 1983– —Juvenile literature. 2. Football players—United States—Biography—Juvenile literature. 3. Quarterbacks (Football)—United States—Biography—Juvenile literature. I. Title.
GV939.R6235G34 2013
796.332092—dc23
[B]
                                                                                      2012018305
eBook ISBN: 9781612283982

ABOUT THE AUTHOR: Tammy Gagne is the author of numerous books for both adults and children, including *What It's Like to Be America Ferrera, Day by Day with Beyoncé, We Visit Mexico, Ways to Help Chronically Ill Children,* and *How to Convince Your Parents You Can Care for A Pet Racing Pigeon* for Mitchell Lane Publishers. As an avid volunteer, one of her favorite pastimes is visiting schools to speak to kids about the writing process. She lives in northern New England with her husband, son, dogs, and parrots.

PUBLISHER'S NOTE: The following story has been thoroughly researched and to the best of our knowledge represents a true story. While every possible effort has been made to ensure accuracy, the publisher will not assume liability for damages caused by inaccuracies in the data, and makes no warranty on the accuracy of the information contained herein. This story has not been authorized or endorsed by Aaron Rodgers.

TABLE OF CONTENTS

Words in **bold** type can be found in the glossary.

The staff at Pleasant Valley High School in Chico, California is very proud of their former student, Aaron Rodgers. The school even changed its colors for the day on February 4, 2011 from blue and white to green and gold to celebrate Aaron and his Green Bay Packers teammates. The team had just earned a spot in Super Bowl XLV. Two days later the Packers won the game with a final score of 31-25.

No Full Ride

Imagine the thrill of being offered a full college **scholarship** (SKOL-er-ship) in exchange for doing something you love. Very few high school seniors get this chance. Those who do get this opportunity often make a name for themselves as professional athletes. Many athletes today even credit their *full ride* as the event that made their pro career possible.

When Aaron Rodgers looks back on his high school days, though, he has no such memory. After Aaron graduated from Pleasant Valley High School in 2002, not a single Division I college offered him a scholarship. So how did he become the household name that he is today?

Aaron grew up as the middle child of Ed and Darla Rodgers' three sons. He was born in Chico, California on December 2, 1983. Watching football was a family pastime for the Rodgers household. Aaron started watching when he was just two years old. He had a basic understanding of **statistics** by the time he entered kindergarten.

Aaron's family shares his passion for football. Here (from left to right) his brother Jordan, father Ed, mother Darla, grandmother Barbara, and grandfather Chuck share a moment with Aaron just after he had been named Most Valuable Player in Super Bowl XLV.

As a young boy, Aaron played many sports, but football was his favorite. His father had played football in college, and semi-pro football after he graduated. Aaron had inherited his father's talent and passion for the game. Aaron knew what needed to be done on the field, and he had no trouble expressing these thoughts to his teammates.

As Aaron moved on to high school, he excelled both on and off the field. During his senior year, his passes totaled 2,176 yards. This number broke the school record. Aaron also earned A's in most of his classes and scored very high on the SAT, a test that many colleges use to decide who they will accept.

He seemed like the perfect candidate for a college football scholarship. Unfortunately, Aaron was the single star on the Pleasant Valley High School football team. Few Division I **scouts** were interested in players from losing teams. With no one offering Aaron a free education, he decided to attend Butte (BYOOT) College, a junior college in nearby Oroville, California.

Aaron joined the University of California Golden Bears after playing a single season with the Butte Roadrunners. As just a sophomore, he became the team's starting quarterback by the fourth game of the season.

The Road to the NFL

Butte was a small school, but it did have a football program. The college had also produced one **alumnus** who had gone on to a successful NFL career. When Aaron entered Butte, Larry Allen was a guard for the Dallas Cowboys. Allen played a total of 12 seasons for this team, and even earned a Super Bowl ring during one of them.

Aaron would be starting his college football career on the same team as Allen had: the Roadrunners. During his freshman year at Butte, Aaron and the Roadrunners won 10 out of 11 games in the NorCal Conference. He threw a total of 26 touchdowns. Aaron was finally part of a successful team. The Roadrunners ended up winning the conference championship and finished as the number two junior college team in the nation.

The Roadrunners' winning season caught the eye of coach Jeff Tedford of the University of California. He came to Oroville to watch the team practice. Before he even got back home, he had called to offer Aaron a scholarship. Most junior college players have to play for two seasons before joining a Division I team, but Aaron's hard work in his classes changed that. His good grades in high school, combined with his high SAT scores, made it possible for him to join the Golden Bears after just a single year at Butte.

In 2003, Aaron began his sophomore year at the University of California on the bench as the backup quarterback. But once again, all he needed was a chance to prove his talents. Aaron became the starting quarterback after the

Bears' fourth game. He went on to complete 61.6 percent of his passes for 2,903 yards and to throw for 19 touchdown passes. The following year he raised his **completion rate** to 66.1 percent, throwing for 2,566 yards and 24 touchdowns.

In 2005, Aaron decided to take a big chance. Most football players play in college for four years, but he declared himself eligible for the NFL draft after just three years. He knew that there weren't many good quarterbacks among the contenders that year. The San Francisco 49ers were looking for a passer, but coach Mike Nolan ended up passing on Aaron. The team chose Alex Smith instead.

Aaron was hopeful that one of the other teams would choose him. He and Smith had been the top two quarterbacks among all the contenders. Still, team after team overlooked him. After 23 other players were selected, the Green Bay Packers made their move, and they chose Aaron with the 24th pick. He had finally made it to the NFL. As with everything else in his football career, though, it wasn't anything like he imagined it would be.

Aaron poses with the Green Bay Packers' general manager, Ted Thompson, in 2005. Aaron had taken a big chance by declaring himself eligible for the NFL draft as a college junior. The risk paid off when the the Packers selected him with the 24th pick.

Waiting for His Chance

The Green Bay Packers already had a star quarterback. His name was Brett Favre. Aaron thought that joining the team would mean spending a lot of time on the bench again, and he was right. It seemed the Packers were grooming him to take over for Favre someday, but no one knew when that would be.

Aaron's first year on the team proved to be a difficult one for everyone. Multiple team members suffered injuries. Some took players out for the remainder of the 2005 season. The Packers had quickly gone from winning three division championships in a row to losing games by double digits to poorly-ranked teams. Aaron played in just three games. He completed 9 of 16 passes for 65 yards.

CHAPTER THREE

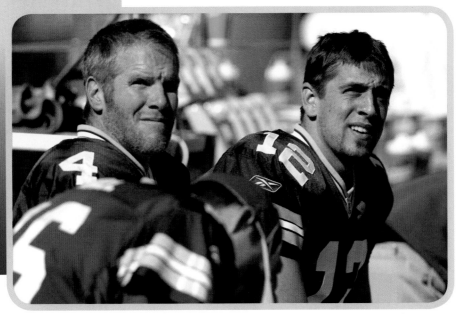

The 2005 season was a tough one for the Green Bay Packers. There were a few highlights, however. Here Brett Favre and Aaron Rodgers take a breath during a game against the New Orleans Saints on October 9, 2005. The Packers won the game with a final score of 52-3.

His second year with the Packers was even worse. Favre had been talking about retiring, but he decided to stay on at the last minute. As if sitting on the bench hadn't been bad enough, Aaron then suffered a broken foot in a game the Packers lost to the New England Patriots, 35-0. This time it was Aaron who was out for the remainder of the season.

It was looking like Aaron's time with the Packers was coming to an end as the 2007 draft neared. Many people thought the Packers were going to send Aaron to the Oakland

Raiders in exchange for Randy Moss. In the end, though, it was the Patriots who traded for Moss, and Aaron would stay put for now.

Prior to the 2007 season, there was a lot of talk that this year would be the year that Favre would retire. It seemed that Aaron would get his chance to prove what he could do on the field. But in February, Favre announced that he would return to the Packers again. The whole situation quickly turned into a joke among sports reporters.

But in November, in a game against the Cowboys, Aaron got his chance to prove his worth. Favre was injured in the second quarter, and Aaron stepped in, throwing for 201 yards. The next game, Favre returned and continued to play through to the end of the Packers' 2007 season. It was becoming clearer to everyone, though, that he was no longer the force he once was. In the NFC Championship game against the New York Giants, he threw an **interception** in overtime. The Giants won the game moments later with a field goal. Favre's interception had cost the team their shot at the Super Bowl.

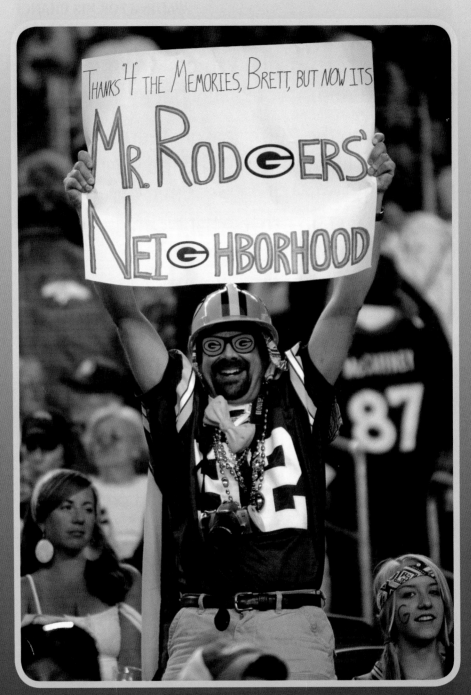

Aaron's fans cheered him on when he became the new starting quarterback for the Green Bay Packers in 2008. The 2008 season proved to be better than previous seasons, but Aaron still had progress to make. He won many games, but he also lost some by just a touchdown or less.

Good, Better, Best

In March of 2008, Brett Favre announced yet again that he was going to retire from football. Most people believed him, but a few waited for him to change his mind. And he did just that in June, before training camp began. By this time, though, coach Mike McCarthy had decided it was time for a change. The Packers traded Favre to the New York Jets.

Aaron's first season as the starting quarterback for the Packers was a good one, but not a great one. He led the team to victories over the Detroit Lions, Seattle Seahawks, and Indianapolis Colts. He threw for more than 4,000 yards and 28 touchdowns. Unfortunately, his inexperience led to losses by just a touchdown or less in seven games. His

Here Aaron and teammate Scott Wells get ready for the snap in their game against the Detroit Lions in Green Bay, Wisconsin on December 28, 2008. The Packers defeated the Lions with a final score of 31-21.

biggest weakness seemed to be staying strong in close games.

By 2009, Aaron was learning to come through for his team, even in tight games. He started the season with a 50-yard pass in the last minute of a game against the Chicago Bears. Aaron and the Packers ended the season with 11 wins and 5 losses. He threw for 4,434 yards, scoring 30 touchdowns for his team. These numbers placed him near the top of the NFC.

As Aaron had already learned, nothing worth having was going to come easy. This didn't change in 2010. Although the season started off with several wins, Aaron later suffered two **concussions**. He even had to sit out an entire game due to one of them. But Aaron was no stranger to obstacles, and he came back with a vengeance that led the Packers all the way to Super Bowl XLV.

If Aaron had ever earned himself an opportunity to prove himself on the field, the 2011 Super Bowl was it. The first half against the Pittsburgh Steelers came to an end with a

By 2009, Aaron was defeating other teams even in tight games. Here he smiles after throwing the winning touchdown in a game against the Chicago Bears on September 13, 2009. The Green Bay Packers won the game with a final score of 21-15.

Teammates Clay Matthews and Aaron Rodgers celebrate their Super Bowl XLV win against the Pittsburgh Steelers. The Green Bay Packers had to work hard in the third and fourth quarters for the win. In the end, though, they were the ones holding the Lombardi Trophy.

score of 21 to 10, Green Bay. It seemed like it was going to be an easy one for the Packers. The next quarter, though, was a whole different ball game, quite literally. The Steelers were not going down without a fight. In the third quarter, Pittsburgh narrowed Green Bay's lead to only 4 points. It all rested on the final quarter. No longer frazzled by close games, Aaron delivered one solid pass after another—until the Packers won the game, 31 to 25. After the game was over, Aaron was named the Super Bowl Most Valuable Player.

It has become a common phrase for famous athletes to shout immediately after winning important games. When asked what they will do next, they proclaim, "I'm going to Disney World!" In 2011 Aaron Rodgers earned his right to say these familiar words. Here he rides alongside Mickey Mouse the day after the Green Bay Packers beat the Pittsburgh Steelers in Super Bowl XLV.

CHAPTER FIVE

Lessons Learned

Today Aaron Rodgers is considered one of the best quarterbacks in the NFL. Overnight success stories may be inspiring, but there are lessons to be learned from stories like Aaron's as well. The most important of these is to never give up on your dreams.

Aaron's belief in himself was one of the biggest reasons he was able to succeed. He told *Sports Illustrated,* "I never doubted I could do this. I just always wondered if I'd get a chance. I knew I had the ability. The question was, when would I get to show it?"

While Aaron waited, he also had to endure his share of rejection and humiliation along the way. Being selected 24th in the 2005 NFL draft

Aaron Rodgers had come a long way when he and the Green Bay Packers won Super Bowl XLV. After being passed over by 21 teams in the 2005 NFL draft, he was now the Most Valuable Player of the Super Bowl Champions in 2011.

was especially tough for him. "I was passed over by 21 teams," he reminded his fans in *Sports Illustrated Kids.* "[But I] still didn't listen to the doubters who said I wasn't tall enough, didn't have a strong enough arm, didn't throw a good enough deep ball, I waited my turn."

"The one lesson I learned," Aaron went on to share in *Sports Illustrated Kids,* "is opportunity is going to come knocking at some point. Whenever [they] come up, you've got to make the most of them."

ESPN's Ron Jaworski told *Sporting News,* "I love the way Aaron has developed. To me it's kind of the old school way, the way it used to be done. You get a young quarterback with a lot

In the offseason Aaron Rodgers enjoys playing games other than football. Here he lends a hand in the Fourth Annual Donald Driver Charity Softball Game at Fox Cities Stadium in Appleton, Wisconsin. Packers offense played against Packers defense in the event. Aaron caught the ball that ended the sixth inning, but by the bottom of the ninth, the defense had won the game 18-16.

Aaron and his teammates B.J. Coleman and Graham Harrell get ready for the upcoming season at NFL football minicamp in Green Bay, Wisconsin on June 12, 2012.

As a player on the 2012 NFC Pro Bowl team, Aaron signs autographs for his fans following Pro Bowl practice in Honolulu, Hawaii.

of talent, and before he goes on the field you let him learn the game. And that's what he was able to do."

Aaron Rodgers is living proof that good things come to those who wait, and his story is far from over. As Green Bay Packers general manager Ted Thompson told *Sporting News,* "He is still growing, still getting better. I think we'll be able to write all the history about him 10, 12, or 15 years from now."

CAREER STATISTICS

Year	Team	G	Att	Comp	Pct	Yds	TD	Int	Lng	Rate
2011	Green Bay Packers	15	502	343	68.3	4,643	45	6	93	122.5
2010	Green Bay Packers	15	475	312	65.7	3,922	28	11	86	101.2
2009	Green Bay Packers	16	541	350	64.7	4,434	30	7	83	103.2
2008	Green Bay Packers	16	536	341	63.6	4,038	28	13	71	93.8
2007	Green Bay Packers	2	28	20	71.4	218	1	0	43	106.0
2006	Green Bay Packers	2	15	6	40.0	46	0	0	16	48.2
2005	Green Bay Packers	3	16	9	56.3	65	0	1	16	39.8
TOTAL		69	2,113	1,381	65.4	17,366	132	38	93	104.1

G=Games played; Att=Attempts; Comp=Completions; Pct=Percentage; Yds=Yards;
TD=Touchdowns; Int=Interceptions; Lng=Longest Pass; Rate=Quarterback Rating

CHRONOLOGY

1983   Aaron Rodgers is born on December 2 in Chico, California.

2002   Graduates from Pleasant Valley High School, with no scholarship offers. Later this year, he enrolls in Butte College in Oroville, California.

2003   Wins the NorCal Conference Championship as a member of the Butte Roadrunners. The team finishes as the number two junior college team in the nation. Aaron begins his sophomore year at the University of California.

2005   Declares himself eligible for the NFL draft pick. He is the 24th player chosen, becoming a member of the Green Bay Packers.

2008   After announcing his retirement several times, Brett Favre tries to change his mind again. Ultimately, the Packers trade him to the New York Jets, making Aaron the starting quarterback for the team.

2010   The Packers finish their 2009-2010 season with 11 wins and 5 losses.

2011   Aaron and the Green Bay Packers win Super Bowl XLV against the Pittsburgh Steelers with a score of 31 to 25.

FIND OUT MORE

Books

Reischel, Rob. *Aaron Rodgers: Leader of the Pack.* Chicago, Illinois: Triumph Books, 2011.

Savage, Jeff. *Aaron Rodgers (Amazing Athletes).* Minneapolis, Minnesota: Lerner Classroom, 2011.

Works Consulted

Crouse, Karen. "Packers' Rodgers Has Deep Roots in Chico." *The New York Times,* January 30, 2011.

Dillon, Dennis. "Worth the Wait: Super Bowl XLV." *Sporting News,* February 14, 2011.

King, Peter. "Pack Where They Belong." *Sports Illustrated,* January 31, 2011.

McGinn, Bob. "Brett Who?" *Sports Illustrated Kids,* September 2009.

On the Internet

Green Bay Packers Official Website
http://www.packers.com/team/roster/Aaron-Rodgers/fe1a862d-b24a-4123-b43e-c116b59395cc

Sports Illustrated: Aaron Rodgers
http://sportsillustrated.cnn.com/football/nfl/players/7200/index.html

Web/Videos

"Jeff Tedford talks about Aaron Rodgers."
http://www.youtube.com/watch?v=I8184E45_0E

GLOSSARY

alumnus (uh-LUHM-nuhs)—A graduated student of a college or university.

completion rate (kuhm-PLEE-shuhn REYT)—The percentage of a quarterback's passes that are caught; a 61 percent completion rate means that for every 100 passes a quarterback throws, 61 are caught, or completed.

concussion (kuhn-KUHSH-uhn)—An injury to a person's brain or spinal cord due to a jarring impact.

interception (in-ter-SEP-shuhn)—The act of a football pass being caught by the defense of the opposing team.

scholarship (SKOL-er-ship)—A sum of money given to a student to use for school tuition, usually based on his or her achievement in academics or sports.

scout (SKOUT)—A person who travels to find new players and bring them to their team.

statistics (sta-TIS-tiks)—The collection and study of numbers, such as sports scores, used to assess past performance and predict future success.

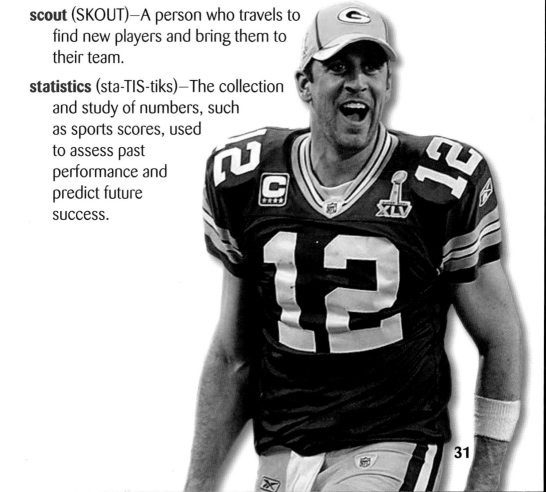

INDEX